Travel like Us

A TRAVEL GUIDE BASED ON OUR EXPERIENCES ACROSS THE WORLD

FROM ATHAN AND ATHENA KARAMEROS

Jason Karameros

TRAVEL LIKE US

FOLLOW @ATHANANDATHENA ON INSTAGRAM

Charleston, SC
www.PalmettoPublishing.com

Travel Like Us
Copyright © 2021 by J. Karameros

First Edition

Paperback ISBN: 978-1-64990-879-7
eBook ISBN: 978-1-64990-880-3

TABLE OF CONTENTS

COVID Talk   ix

Introduction from Athan and Athena   xiii

Chapter One: Book in Advance   1

Chapter Two: Little Trip-Bits   3

Chapter Three: Research Pays!   5

Chapter Four: You Know You're a Tourist When…   12

Chapter Five: Go Where the Prices Say   14

Chapter Six: It's All about Value   17

Chapter Seven: Don't Spend Your Vacation on Lines   21

Chapter Eight: What Diet?   24

Chapter Nine: Holiday, Holiday   26

Chapter Ten: Try Multiple Sites   29

Chapter Eleven: Sometimes You Gotta Splurge I   31

Chapter Twelve: Airline Mileage, Hotel Points, Etc.…   36

Chapter Thirteen: Use Airline Lounges   38

Chapter Fourteen: You Want a Travel Tip? Tip!   42

Chapter Fifteen: If Something Is Wrong, Speak Up!   45

Chapter Sixteen: Sometimes You Gotta Splurge II   50

Chapter Seventeen: Travel with Kids   53

Chapter Eighteen: Eating Right   63

Chapter Nineteen: Sometimes You Gotta Splurge III   72

Chapter Twenty: Beware the Night (Flights)   76

Chapter Twenty-One: European Travel   79

Chapter Twenty-Two: Red Light & Red Flags   85

Chapter Twenty-Three: Don't Get Taken at Your Hotel   88

Chapter Twenty-Four: Casinos   91

Chapter Twenty-Five: Where Are the Lawyers?   93

Chapter Twenty-Six: Crime, Corruption, and Terrorism   95

Chapter Twenty-Seven: Travel[ed] like Us in Mexico   99

Chapter Twenty-Eight: Post-COVID   102

COVID Talk

COVID-19 has changed the world. In addition to the obvious pain, suffering, and death, it has devastated the economies of many nations and individuals. The travel industry has been extremely hard hit. Airlines, restaurants, hotels, entire countries, and so many individuals who rely on tourism for their economic lifeblood have been struggling or slowly dying.

In late February to early March 2020, my wife and I were lucky enough to go on a combination of tenth anniversary and friend's fiftieth birthday trip to Marrakesh, Morocco. At this point, there were growing concerns about COVID, and the airports in Europe were only half filled with people, some wearing masks. People were concerned, but nobody was sure of what was to come.

The trip turned out to be great, but less than two weeks later, New York City went into a lockdown for months. Our family thankfully did not get sick, but we were very strict in our lockdown. After many quarantined months, we enjoyed our first restaurant dinner outside in late May in Pennsylvania with the kids' grandparents, whom we hadn't seen in months.

We decided to take a summer road trip to Virginia and South Carolina instead of flying in the uncertain times. The COVID rates were very low down South, and people weren't even wearing masks at that point. It was on that trip that we finally had our first indoor restaurant meal since the lockdown started. We kept our masks on and were socially distant, even from our close friends, as we mutually enjoyed the beach on July 4th.

Our planned summer trip to Europe with a number of friends and family to celebrate my fiftieth birthday had to be canceled. Thankfully we received full refunds for most of the expenses. We had booked another birthday getaway in August to the Dominican Republic, but then we had to cancel that trip as COVID rates rose there. We settled on a getaway to beautiful Newport, Rhode Island, instead, another road trip. That trip was great as it was the first break for two of our close friends, both first responders from New York City.

The world changed, and travel did with it. Hotels weren't doing daily cleaning unless you requested it. Dirty towels were left outside the door along with the trash. You needed reserved times to use the pool. Buffet breakfasts were stopped.

Hopefully with vaccines becoming more available, the world can go back to some sort of "normal." However, cleaner airplanes, wearing masks, and sanitizing hands to minimize spreading germs are hopefully things that will stay in place and help the travel industry come back strong.

This book is for travelers of all ages and all types of budgets. It's about being wise when you travel and finding the best deals, no matter what your budget is. We want you to learn as we did through our experiences.

If you can:
Explore…Go out to eat…Be safe…And
Travel like Us

Jason Karameros

Introduction from Athan and Athena

Our dad loves to travel; he has a condition described by a fancy word called wanderlust. He lived in Korea and has been to Europe many, many times. Our mom also loves to travel. She was on airplanes when she was a baby, flying all around Asia and coming back and forth to New York. Each of them has been to five continents.

My sister, Ryan Athena, is two years younger than me, so she has fewer trips than I do, but we have been traveling since I can remember. Here's what we've learned so far...

CHAPTER ONE

Book in Advance

A lot of times, our dad will tell me that we have 120 more big sleeps (nights) before our trip to ……

That's a lot of big sleeps, and sometimes it's even more big sleeps than 120! He always books our vacations ahead of time. It costs a lot less money to do it that way. Hotels and flights are usually much cheaper when booked in advance. Another benefit of booking early is that the trip can hopefully be paid for before you go. That way, whatever money you need to spend while away will only be expenses like food and fun things.

Our cousin travels a lot with his family too, but they always book things at the last minute. They wind up paying a lot more money or looking for cheap deals that may have some problems. One time, he was going to Cancún, and he booked a "cheap" last-minute trip on a charter airline; let's call it *Scare Air*. The problem with *Scare Air*, aside from no customer service, horrible reviews, and questionable products, is that they only had one plane. Our hard-working cousin based an entire trip on a company that was not reliable.

So when the plane was grounded because they didn't have certain parts (knowing this company, it might have been the wings), our cousin's trip was ruined. Book in advance with reputable airlines and hotels!

Athan and Athena

CHAPTER TWO

Little Trip-Bits

- If going abroad, make sure that you buy a travel adapter that works in the areas that you will be going to.
- If you plan on renting a car, find out if you need to get an International Driver's License - (easy to get at American Automobile Association).
- It can be easier to get foreign currency while you're still here. You can order it through your bank, and the rates are usually cheaper.
- If needed, give travel notification to your credit cards. Sometimes the security on your cards, especially at smaller banks, might think your foreign spending is fraudulent.
- Do that for your ATM card as well.

- When looking for airline tickets, maybe go open-jaw—fly into one city and home from another; it can save money or time at the very least.

- If you have kids, bring a few of their favorite snacks just in case you're going somewhere where they may not have them.

- And speaking of kids and snacks, here's a reminder: let trips be a snack heaven for the kids. Let them splurge, not to the point of being sick or anything, but definitely indulge them a bit more. It will make them like traveling more and it will make your journey, and that of your neighbors onboard, much better and usually quieter.

Athan and Athena

Research Pays!

I know that we generally don't like school. (But the Keswell School rocks!) I know vacations and travel shouldn't be associated with homework, but don't you want to enjoy your trip to the fullest?

Now you can go to the travel section of the nearest bookstore and buy every travel book ever written on a particular place and strategically place them around your residence so that you can scoop up some knowledge at any dull moment. You can also go to the nearest computer and research from a number of websites on any destination that you're interested in.

But let's just say that you don't want to do any of that. You don't have to. Today it's so easy. Go on YouTube. Search for a travel video on the place you're going to. They're usually from five to ten minutes long. Some are way better than others, but many will give you some great spots to see. They will give a super quick look at the culture and food. They will show you that Greeks eat a lot of lamb and fish. They will tell you that Italy is not the place to go for a no-carb diet. Take a quick look so you know that when you're somewhere that you may only travel to one time, you don't miss something special while you're there.

Another reason why research is so important is that you can potentially save thousands of dollars and greatly increase the quality of your trip.

In 2014, my family prepared to take a trip to the Philippines. This was a very important trip for us. My mom was born there, and she has a large family who still lives there. Also many of our relatives who live in the US were going to go back as it was a special occasion. Our great-uncle and aunt were renewing their vows for their fiftieth wedding anniversary in the same church that they were originally married at in Manila, the capital of the Philippines.

These were going to be the longest flights of our lives. It usually takes two days to get to the Philippines from New York City. Because of the international date line, when you leave New York City on a Tuesday afternoon, you get to Manila around one o'clock on Thursday morning, assuming you change planes.

This was obviously a very special trip for our family, and my parents wanted to plan accordingly. I was going to turn four on the trip, and my sister was going to turn two—we have summer birthdays. And that made a big difference for the trip. Since these flights were so long, my parents decided that it was worth the splurge to business class tickets since we would have full beds on the flights. Many airlines offer discounted tickets in business class for children under the age of eleven, so my parents shopped around.

Another very important factor was that Athena was going to turn two while we were on the trip. Typically, airlines will allow children under two to fly for free (or a small fee) as a lap child, meaning the infant would not take up a seat and be on the parent's lap. Since Athena was turning two on the trip, many airlines wanted to charge her the children's rate and demanded that my parents bought a seat for her since she would be two within the time of the trip. Since this was business class, this meant close to $2,800 extra.

Now this is where research comes into play. By checking out a few sites, and even talking directly to the airline, my dad found out that Korean Air would still consider Athena a lap child for the whole trip. That meant we only needed to purchase three business class seats instead of four, saving $2,800 at the time. Additionally, with more research, my dad used some websites to look at the seating of the plane and which seats were available. He strategically chose our seats, hoping that where they were would dissuade a solo business traveler from sitting in between occupied seats in the hopes that we would have an empty business class seat between us. It worked!

So for the fourteen-hour-plus trip from Los Angeles to Seoul, we each had our own full-size bed on the plane. And we also had the same setup for the over five-hour trip from Seoul to Manila. We used the same strategy for the flights back home. We had decided to go from New York City to Los Angeles first and stay a few days at the beach to break the trip up—we used airline miles to get to Los Angeles and back for free and got much better business prices from Los Angeles to Manila than from New York City.

My mom held Athena at times but could put her into the unoccupied seat next to her for the rest of the time. Even my mom was impressed with how much space there was on the plane. When we first boarded, she did jumping jacks in front of her seat to show how much room there was between the seats. My dad may have annoyed my mom a little with all the research he was doing, but in the end, we were all super happy, and the trip was an amazing adventure in Asia. Research pays!

Athan

Don't even think of sitting in that open seat! It's mine as soon as the cabin doors close!

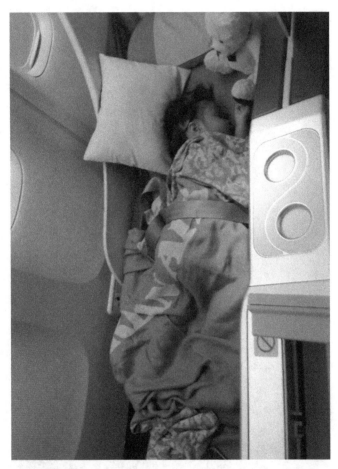

The research worked! Good night, everyone. Wake me for ice cream when we're close to landing. Free seat for me! $2,800 more for my parents!

These seats that turned into beds really helped with the forty hours of flight times on the trip. My friend Stitch the Bear really appreciated it!

You Know You're a Tourist When...

- you're walking so slow that you're hindering the locals from doing their thing.
- you're wearing a rain poncho, and most likely it's not even raining.
- you're eating in a restaurant surrounded by other tourists.
- you're bumping into people because you're walking around with your head in a pull-out map or on Google Maps on your phone.
- you're waiting on a giant line to get into an attraction when there were definitely other ways to get into the place without the line.
- you're saying FOREIGN WORDS REALLY LOUDLY, thinking it helps with understanding.

- you're eating fast food from a chain restaurant despite being thousands of miles from home.
- you're too busy taking pictures so you can remember the sight instead of actually looking at the sight and appreciating it. (Even many non-tourists are guilty of this one.)
- you're eating in a foreign restaurant that has a sign outside advertising its "tourist menu" in English.

Athan and Athena

CHAPTER FIVE

Go Where the Prices Say

When my sister and I were younger, my dad was nervous about us traveling on long flights. I am autistic, and my dad worries about how I might react to certain things. Because of that, sometimes we flew to places and got beds on the plane in business class. My dad said we can't do it all the time because it costs a lot of money.

But we still manage to do it when the price is right. One year my mom and dad were looking to take us on a family trip to France. My dad kept looking, but he said it was very expensive; however, when he changed his search to Spain, the same business class seats that were over $3,000 a person to France became $1,400 a person to Spain. So we happily went to Spain and got to sleep on full beds for the overnight flight there and the longer flight back home!

Another time, we wanted to go to a beach destination for a few days over Thanksgiving. Apparently we weren't the only ones; tickets from New York City to San Juan, Puerto Rico, were about $700-$800 per person (the roundtrip fares are each normally between $150-$500), so my dad said that it was too much money for us to go.

He kept looking and found tickets from New York City to Paris, France, for the same days as the Puerto Rico trip at about $450 each for premium economy (these roundtrip fares are each normally between $1,000-$2,100). So for the four of us, the air was $1800 to France instead of $2,800 to Puerto Rico. Plus the flight to France travels further for a longer time, and we were in premium economy—bigger seats, more bags, and better service.

On Thanksgiving Day, we had our holiday lunch at a restaurant upstairs in the Eiffel Tower! And we had duck instead of turkey, but I was happy that we went. I fell in love with Paris and as Athena still screams it, "THE EIFFEL TOWER."

Athan

It's All about Value

Value is an important concept. Value your time and money. For time, understand that time is money. Many of you work by the hour, but even if you don't, you know you don't want to spend time at your workplace when you don't have to. Unfortunately, many travelers don't think the same way. A lot of people are willing to waste hours for a few extra dollars in savings, but let's really examine this in detail.

My dad went down to Charleston, South Carolina from New York City to meet up with a group of friends. One of the friends, Vincenzo, was also flying from the New York area, but he didn't arrive until very late that night. When they were out, my dad asked him what took him so long. It turned out that Vincenzo booked a cheaper flight from Newark (a New York City area airport) that connected to Charleston via Detroit.

My dad was a little confused. Instead of taking a one-hour-and-fifteen-minute direct flight, Vincenzo flew about the same distance west instead of south. Then he had to kill two hours in the Detroit airport. *Then* he flew the one hour and forty minutes to Charleston. So he got on one plane in Newark and was in Charleston about five hours later, whereas my dad was there for about four hours before Vincenzo.

Was the $70 difference in the flight price for this leg worth the extra four hours? Maybe. Keep in mind that Vincenzo also had to kill time in Detroit, spending money on food and drinks there. Also when you switch flights, you have a greater chance that your luggage will get lost. So if you worked hard to earn vacation time, it's usually better to spend that time on vacation, not stuck in an airport or taking extra flights. Go get that little drink with the umbrella in it; you deserve it!

My yummy kids' meal in premium economy from Germany.

Likewise think about value when you think about flying in premium economy or business class. Sometimes, premium economy is about $120 per ticket more for a trip than economy is. Let's say that flight is eight hours long. So ask yourself, is it worth $15 more per hour to have more legroom and more recline on an eight-hour trip? For some people, it might not be. But if you can afford it, are tall, and value sleep, it very well might be. Just make sure you think about it. Look at my previous photo: better food and extra space mean people can actually sleep!

Athena

CHAPTER SEVEN

Don't Spend Your Vacation on Lines

You're standing on a line that has no start and no end. You're barely moving. You've been there for fifty minutes already and you don't know how much longer it will be. You're sweating in the oppressive Italian sun because you have no shade. Do you really need to see Botticelli's *Birth of Venus* in person? When you or your kids need a bathroom, you have to beg the clerk at the coffee shop in broken Italian until he makes you buy an espresso so you can use the toilet. As you stand there, the sweat finds its way into your eyes until the saltiness makes your eyes hurt. Then as your eyes clear, you see them—a family, fresh as the spring air, casually saunters on by. They look at all the people in line and happily revel in the fact that they're not on that line. They stroll to the door of the museum, and a wave of air-conditioned air relieves them of the oppression outside as they calmly collect their tickets or show their passes and begin their visit.

Admit it. We hate them. What happened? What happened was that this family did a little research. The Uffizi Gallery in Florence and the Louvre Museum in Paris are just two of the many examples of museums that have amazingly long lines, but also have ways to beat those lines. For the Uffizi, a simple online rebooking can get you and your family timed ticket entries with no wait. And in Paris, there are a number of multiday tourist cards that provide a similar key. Sometimes there is no extra fee, other times there might be a minor charge.

Time is a value in and of itself on a vacation. Don't waste it standing on a line when you don't need to be. Especially post COVID, check the museum's website and research!

Athan and Athena

No line for us at the Pompidou Museum in Paris on this cold November day!

CHAPTER EIGHT

What Diet?

If you're going on vacation, you should not deprive your-self. Eat pasta and pizza in Italy. Eat rice and noodles in Asia. Eat sweets from exotic locales. While you're doing this, one thing to think about is whether you want to bring home an extra ten pounds as a souvenir from a great vacation.

How can you minimize the weight gain while still enjoying yourself? Here are a few things:

Exercise when you're away. Do whatever you can. Go for a morning run or walk. Swim laps in the pool or at the beach. Hit the hotel gym. If it doesn't have one, find out about day passes at local gyms. Even spending the whole day walking and seeing sights will burn a lot more energy than most of us are used to, so that can be a good way to keep the fat off.

Eat heavy earlier in the day. Maybe have a big breakfast, smaller lunch, and even smaller dinner. Or another thing you can do is to enjoy your breakfast and a big lunch, maybe an early light tapas or *aperitivo* snack, and then don't do dinner. Sixteen hour fasts are becoming a big thing in the exercise world. If your last meal is at 3:00 or 4:00 p.m., and you don't eat again until 8:00 a.m., in those sixteen hours your body will be ready to eat after you've burned off a bunch of calories, especially if you add a morning exercise to your routine before your breakfast.

And finally, my parents like to go on diets before the vacation. They like to look better in their bathing suits, so for them, it's nice to lose weight beforehand. Also it makes the vacation more of a reward. By depriving themselves for a time before they go away, it makes all the good food and drink even that much better.

Before a trip to Greece, my dad went two months without any white wine and only a few glasses of red. He did not want to have the carbs and sugars in the wine in an effort to drop some pounds. In his case, the payoff was a number of vineyard tours on our trip to Greece, where he tasted and drank all hues in the spectrum of wines. If you can lose five to six pounds before vacation, then those five to six you may put on while away will just keep you at you.

Athena

CHAPTER NINE

Holiday, Holiday

We have some friends who do not like to travel for the holidays. It's understandable to want to be with family during these times, but why not be with family somewhere different? We have traveled with our grandparents to the Caribbean over Christmas a number of times; we have also visited friends in the US. Other times, we traveled with just our parents.

Obviously the holidays are a good time to travel because we don't have school, and my parents have time off, but we have selfish reasons too. In our case, we get to have more than one Christmas morning. You see, wherever we are, Santa always seems to find us. Our mom always sets up some kind of tree in our hotel room, on the balcony, or outside. It might be a few lights and ribbons, but it definitely gives us the Christmas spirit. And when we go to bed on Christmas Eve, we always find presents for all of us on Christmas morning. And the best part about presents while away is that when we get back home after the trip, our tree at home has *more* presents from Santa, our friends, and family. Traveling at this time is great because Santa gives us 2 sets of gifts, and of course being able to travel is already an amazing gift that we get from our parents.

Also a lot of the places that we go to usually have giant decorated trees and lights on their property, and they often have special activities set up for the holidays. We were just in Mexico for Christmas this past year, and Santa even made it to the beach in his sled that was towed by a Jet Ski from the water. It was awesome! They also had a cool beach hut with a small tree and a fireplace with chairs, where we hung out and took pictures. On Christmas evening, the restaurant had a special feast of the seven fishes menu, and for Christmas Day dinner we had an amazing beachfront barbecue on the sand with live music. It was great.

We love having our friends and family over for the holidays or going to their houses, but it can be fun to miss the at-home party every so often to be somewhere new and get the double-up in gifts from Santa.

Likewise for Thanksgiving break, we try to travel somewhere as a family. Domestic airports and roads are crowded, so it's a great time to travel to Europe, especially if you live near the East Coast. If you want to do a short but memorable trip, leave on a Monday or Tuesday night. Most flights to Europe from the East Coast are overnight flights. You can leave in the evening after school, have dinner at the airport or on the plane, and then sleep for a few hours. When you wake up, you're in Europe.

One benefit of trips like this is that they're much cheaper. Most Americans are traveling around the States to see family. Why not change it up every few years by going abroad? They may not have turkey everywhere, but I'm sure you can find something you like. On trips like this, do not travel to more than one city. If you leave on a Tuesday night, you can get to Europe on a Wednesday morning with a Sunday return. That plan gives you four full days in a city. Since you have a limited number of days, don't waste the hours away in a car or train. Get to the hotel, unpack, and go explore your city.

With the time change, your return flight on Sunday morning or early afternoon will get you home so you still can settle in on Sunday evening before returning to school and work on Monday. You might be a little jet-lagged, but memories of having a gelato in Rome can make the jet lag a bit milder.

Athan and Athena

CHAPTER TEN

Try Multiple Sites

Loyalty is an admirable quality, but in the world of travel you should look for the best deals. Some people swear by Expedia, some by Priceline, others Kayak, etc. The bottom line is that you should check multiple sites to get the best deals. Sites like Kayak are great because they're consolidators, pulling together information and rates from multiple other sites. But even sites like these sometimes miss things, and it can be cheaper to go directly to other sites. Sometimes the savings can be a few dollars, other times hundreds.

Even the device to check the deals might matter. When heading on a two night trip to Sarasota, Florida, Dad shopped around on his laptop for some hotel options on a bunch of sites. He was debating in this case between a four-star Westin and a five-star Ritz-Carlton. That debate was before the costs came into play. The Ritz was over $450 a night, which was actually a good deal considering those rooms often go for $600 a night. The Westin was in the $230 range. Right before he was ready to book, Mom checked her iPhone for the Ritz-Carlton price. On her phone, she could book a special rate for $300 a night. On the same site on his computer, that offer did not exist. So they booked it on the phone, and Dad got a few days of value at a fantastic property.

And today we just booked a trip to Mexico on Expedia that was priced $1,600 higher on another website that is usually our cheapest option. Don't take prices for granted. Value and research!

Athan and Athena

CHAPTER ELEVEN

Sometimes You Gotta Splurge I

One of the biggest challenges that airlines have is to keep the customer (you and me) entertained in the air. They need to take up our time to distract us. The way they do this is pretty standard with slight adjustments depending on the airline and length of flight. When you get up to cruising altitude, they begin a beverage service, sometimes with a snack. Some do a beverage service and then a snack service or vice versa. If you're lucky (or unlucky given some of the airline food selections) they will provide a meal service, etc. They also hopefully have either an in-seat digital TV system, movies, or a full personal entertainment system including games, music, etc. If the airline doesn't have any of these things, you may want to reconsider that airline.

But what if you could get on an airplane and have a meal that takes one to one and a half hours? It could be like an experience at a nice restaurant. Maybe they serve your dinner in courses, like a nice appetizer first...

Here's a nice shrimp selection with a chopped salad and two different kinds of bread. There is also some butter and olive oil. All this is served on actual china. And it was delicious.

Second course was a steak with truffle mashed potatoes and vegetables in wine sauce. It was served about twenty to thirty minutes later.

That was really good—restaurant quality good. Then came the delicious chocolate desert for the third course.

This yummy food almost makes me forget that I'm in a metal tube 40,000 feet above the ground flying at 550 miles per hour.

Now this is clearly not the normal airplane meal, not even the normal meals in business class or first class on some airlines. This meal was served on an overnight flight from New York to Milan, Italy. It took place on one of the top airlines in the world, Emirates Airlines. This trip was for my dad's forty-fifth birthday. We were going to spend three weeks in Italy with a bunch of friends, the highlight being a one week rental of a four-hundred-year-old villa in Tuscany.

Originally, my dad bought premium economy tickets on Alitalia for the four of us. They cost about $6,000 for four tickets. This was definitely already a splurge, but it was a special birthday, and we wanted to be as comfortable as possible considering we would be in the air for a total of about sixteen to twenty hours roundtrip.

But then one of our friends noticed a deal via a Facebook ad. Emirates was having a two-for-one sale in business class. Now this was special. Emirates business class is one of the top rated in the world. The tickets from JFK to Milan can normally run from $3,000 to $7,000, *per ticket* in business; however, with this special, it came out to $8,000 total (for the four of us so $2,000 each) versus what could normally be $12,000-$28,000.

Now my parents did some math, using the concept of value that we talked about before. We would go from five more inches of legroom and a slightly bigger incline in Alitalia to full beds and from food in plastic trays to that meal above. Free lounge access came with the tickets of course; that was great because with Emirates at JFK, you actually can board the plane from their lounge without trudging through the airport. And in business, your luggage comes out first at baggage claim.

Additionally, with Emirates business class, a car service is arranged to take you to the airport and pick you up. Now it's time for me to practice my favorite school subject—Math. Our Uber to JFK would have been about $100; our car in Milan would have been about $220 as we were going to Lake Stresa about forty-five miles from the airport. Coming back, we had another $220 getting to Milan airport and our pickup at JFK to home. So this $540 in taxi and car fees was included in the cost of our tickets. These were also plush rides: Mercedes sedans or private shuttle buses.

So if we factor in all the numbers, a $2,000 upgrade to amazing business class, minus the $540 in cabs and $200 in lounge fees (going and returning) leaves $1,260 to upgrade for four people. So it was $315 per person to upgrade and splurge from Alitalia premium economy to Emirates business class roundtrip. Both flight times added up to about 16.5 hours, so $315 divided by 16.5 came out to about an extra $19 an hour per ticket.

Wow—a lot of math, but was it worth it? Even if you hate math, you don't need to bust out the calculator to figure all of this out. Use your common sense and stay within your means but also recognize a great deal—$8,000 instead of $28,000 that some people pay for the *same* seats! For us, it was a celebration and the math was right!

Happy Birthday Dad! Have a drink! In this case he did, at the onboard bar in the business class section of the plane.

Athena

Airline Mileage, Hotel Points, Etc....

We travel a lot. And we take advantage of loyalty clubs as much as we can. For us, JetBlue Airways is our most-used airline. They're centered in New York City; it's called a hub. They fly all across the US, and they fly across the Caribbean. Every time we fly, we get points. But we also get extra points when we use their credit card. And we get even more points when we book travel as a vacation package on their site.

On one trip we took to Curaçao, we earned eighteen times the money spent in miles because of various promotions. The beautiful end-of-summer trip that we had in Curaçao, in addition to being an amazing and budget-friendly experience, earned us enough points for the family to fly to California five months later.

That trip to Italy that we just talked about in the previous chapter also helped us out. When our parents upgraded to Emirates business class on their splurge, the miles they earned were shared with JetBlue, an Emirates partner airline, and those miles got us free flights to visit our friends down South that Christmas. The same process works for hotels and car rentals, etc. Take a look at which airlines have the best programs and which ones you fly the most. Sometimes one trip can pay for another!

Athan and Athena

CHAPTER THIRTEEN

Use Airline Lounges

One of the nice perks about flying first class or business class is that you get to use airline lounges before your flight. Keep that in mind if you're on the fence about buying that kind of ticket. Thankfully even when we are in the less "fancy seats," we can still use the lounges. Of course it may cost a little money, but it can be worth it.

Let me explain the benefits of the lounges. One underappreciated aspect of the lounges is that their bathrooms are generally less crowded and usually much cleaner than the general ones in the terminals. Some lounge bathrooms even have shower facilities, so if you're transferring in an airport after a long flight, it can be a nice way to freshen up after you were just crammed between two bulky football players who decided not to shower after practice for a seven-hour flight.

On that note, most lounges also remove you from the hectic and loud chaos of the general airport terminal to a climate-controlled sanctuary away from the hustle and bustle. The seats are usually bigger and more comfortable, the Wi-Fi is generally better, and there are usually charging stations all over. Sometimes they even have perks like massages, salons, and sleep areas.

Another benefit is that they have food. This selection can be anything from basic snacks—like pretzels, fruits, and chips—to full buffet spreads, serving hot and cold items. Some plush lounges even have full sit-down meal service with waiters. In most of these lounges, the food is included in your admission. Thus, instead of shelling out a ton of money in the airport for OK food, you can get some OK food included with the lounge access. And occasionally the food can be tasty!

Me at the Emirates Lounge at JFK.

Finally, another big advantage of the lounge is that the beverages are usually free. Yes, free! You do not have to pay $3 plus for a bottle of water or more for juices or $9—$20 for a wine or cocktail. In fact, many lounges have a complete selection of top-shelf liquors for you to pour yourself. They also have a selection of beers and wines. My dad likes a cocktail called a N*egroni*. It's Italian and usually costs from $12—$24 in a bar or restaurant in New York City. It's made with equal parts of gin, vermouth, and the Italian liqueur Campari. We were in the Air France lounge in Paris, and our dad made himself two *Negronis* while we waited for the plane. Our dad is big, and he always says, "Drink responsibly!"

Those drinks and food would have easily cost over $150 for our family in the airport, but that day we were allowed access to the lounge via a company called *Priority Pass*. This service allows access to lounges across the world for a small fee. It's even included in the American Express Platinum card. But even without a service like this, many lounges allow entry for a fee.

Figure out how long you have to kill before the flight, and weigh the cost of entry versus what you would spend in the terminal. And don't forget the monetary value of more quiet space with cleaner bathrooms. Imagine the lounge in the Manila airport in summer! Basic but clean and most importantly, air-conditioned on a day with 90-degree temps and 90 percent humidity.

Athan

You Want a Travel Tip? Tip!

My *papou* (grandfather in Greek) worked as a server for most of his life. He was able to support his family because he worked hard, and people rewarded his effort with tips. Tips play an important part in many people's lives, and in addition to being a reward for good service rendered, they can also be a nice incentive for service to come.

In Europe, the servers work for a salary, but an additional tip can be a friendly reward for good service, and considering the prices of most of the restaurants in Europe in comparison with those in the U.S., the tip and bill will most likely still not be close to damaging your budget. At crowded bars and clubs, tipping your bartenders well, especially if you go to the same one, may make it easier for them to remember your pretty face when you thirstily return through the crowd. In Europe, tipping is so rare the establishments will often have noisemakers for the bartenders to use to signal a tip being left. In the States, generous tipping and a good attitude may result in a friendly buyback.

And before you get into those crowded clubs, if there is a long line outside, a generous tip with a friendly doorman *may* get you past the rope if that is your desire. At the hotel, if there is a concierge, a nice tip may get him or her to call in some favors to get you into that special restaurant or to get tickets for events, etc.

This next tip should be obvious. You're trapped in a flying tube for hours with nowhere to go. It makes sense to treat the people who take care of you well, especially when you're on the ground, since they have the power to remove you from the flight. Flight Attendants (FAs) have a tough job—think restaurant servers with life-and-death training. Be kind; it can pay off.

When the obnoxious person in seat 7C keeps hitting his button because he thinks service is slow, you can sit back with a complimentary wine, even better when smuggled in from business or first class by a kind server who knows that *you know* and acknowledge what kind of tough job he or she has.

Help them out when you can. They're not your babysitters or maids. Stack your trash so it's easy to remove when they come by collecting. Be polite. Have your orders ready. No real need to debate the pasta or chicken course when you're flying a long flight in coach; chances are they will both be pretty bad, but they will occupy your time.

Athena

CHAPTER FIFTEEN

If Something Is Wrong, Speak Up!

My family friends are very smart and reasonable people. We were on a group trip once, and at the end of the trip, the other parents mentioned that something had been wrong in their hotel room the entire time, but they did not mention anything to the staff. The parents were going to post about the issue on Tripadvisor when they got home.

There are many people out there who don't really want to be confrontational or deal with any problems during their vacations. Understandable. But in the end, both the customer and the establishment are getting cheated. The customer is wronged as there is some kind of issue that has affected their stay negatively; the establishment is wronged because there is no way for them to fix the issue if for some reason they're unaware of it.

Sometimes when things go wrong, it's not directly the establishment's fault. On one trip to the Caribbean, we were staying at a beautiful hotel right on a lovely beach. At night, we went to dinner in the hotel at an open-air restaurant that they had, although we were seated inside. During the meal, we saw people outside swatting their hands in the air as they quickly scrambled inside. At the same time, the servers frantically shut the big glass doors. The meal was fine, but when it ended, we had to scramble through a biblical swarm of flying ants all the way back to our room. Thankfully only a dozen or so came into the room when we shut the door and barricaded it with towels. It was that bad.

The next morning, my dad opened the door, and this is what we saw in the hallways. Gross!

These carcasses were gathered in the corner of the hallway. There were thousands more on the walls and throughout the outdoor stairways and gutters. Again, certain instances occur that the hotel has no control over. Given the hotel's condition in the morning, we were happy to spend the day at the beautiful beaches on the other side of the island.

We left at 8:00 a.m. and returned at 4:00 p.m. In that eight-hour time span, we returned to the dead; the insect remnants were still all over the place. It wasn't easy for me. I hate bugs! I know I'm bigger than they are, but they're still scary. And I didn't want to keep walking by them as we spent the rest of the night in the hotel. We packed some light bags and actually checked into another hotel for the night so we could comfortably spend the rest of the evening at clean facilities.

The following afternoon, we returned to the hotel, and it was finally better. Dad scheduled an appointment with the general manager of the hotel. They had a pleasant meeting with each other in which my dad described the situation. He said that the swarm was obviously not the hotel's fault, but its inadequate cleanup, even after nearly twenty hours, was. When people are paying hard-earned money to enjoy time off work, they deserve to get what they pay for. Lizards and tropical bugs are one thing.

Biblical swarms, not so much! And no cleanup after said swarms—definitely not!

The general manager agreed. He not only compensated us for the outside hotel room that we were forced to get, but he also sent a few bottles of wine to the room and a few sweets. For the rest of the stay, our room was always cleaned on time, and he remained at our service for whatever we needed. He was made aware of our disappointment, and his actions were enough to make up for the error in the hotel's response. If we hadn't said anything, we would have been uncomfortable in our surroundings, and it would have put a damper on our trip. Instead, we wound up having a great time all in all. We would all go happily back to that hotel and look forward to doing so.

Great service makes me smile in Boracay, Philippines.

CHAPTER SIXTEEN

Sometimes You Gotta Splurge II

One Christmas, we were traveling to Harbour Island in the Bahamas from New York City. We were going to land in Nassau and take a connecting flight to the island. When we were about to board the plane in New York City, we were told to head back to the waiting area. We heard terrible news! The pilot actually fell between the platforms when getting onto the plane. He dropped more than ten feet. We learned afterward that he was OK, but everyone was worried and the crew especially was concerned about their friend. In that circumstance, the company had to change out the entire crew, so our flight was delayed.

Since we had a connecting flight, my dad called the smaller local airline in the Bahamas. He told them that more than half of the passengers on their flight would now be delayed and that they should consider delaying it. He was told they would assess the matter.

Well, when we got there they had assessed the matter and still let their plane leave. So now we were stuck in Nassau with a prepaid hotel in Harbour Island waiting for us. Since this was a small airline, they did not have many seats or options for us, and they said we could get out on a flight the following day. On this trip, it was the four people in my family, and two other family friends were traveling with us, Tita Rita and Tita Ava (Tita means aunt in Tagalog, the language of the Philippines, and it's a sign of respect to older friends and family.)

If we stayed in Nassau overnight, we would've had to get two hotel rooms during a very busy travel period with very expensive rooms. So what did we do?

The desk clerk at the airline actually suggested it. She said, "Why don't you charter a flight?" My dad looked very surprised. My dad didn't have a lot of money when he grew up, so the idea of chartering a plane seemed very strange to him. He asked the woman how much it would cost. She placed a call to her friend, a charter pilot. He told my dad that it would be $780 for the thirty-minute flight. That was less than the cost of the two hotel rooms for the night, and it would still allow us to enjoy the hotels that we had already paid for on the island.

So, my dad said yes. The pilot said he would be there in fifteen minutes after a quick shower. The six of us walked to the private airport a few minutes away and met the pilot. Dad and the pilot loaded the plane with our bags and we climbed into the small propeller plane. Even though this seems very suspect, this was a legitimate charter company and pilot. Of course my dad had asked at the airport and checked the internet. We got into our six-seat plane, friends sat in the back, Athena sat on my mom's lap, I had a seat, and Dad sat next to the pilot in the front.

The plane was very hot, so we kept the door open before takeoff. We even cruised halfway down the runway with my dad holding the door open to get a breeze in the cabin; the pilot requested it. When we did takeoff, it was a quick and pretty flight to our destination. We got to enjoy the rest of the day with only a few hours of delay. In this case, the splurge of chartering a plane was worth it!

Athan

Travel with Kids

AIRPLANES

Don't be scared of traveling with your kids. In fact, if you can get them used to it early and you teach them the right way, they will be great and look forward to it. In the one-hundred-plus flights that my sister and I have been on, there has only been one bad flight and it happened early.

We were flying back from Italy. We had no problems for most of the eight-hour-plus flight home. My four year old body clock thought it was 11:00 p.m., so I was exhausted. I finally fell asleep in my seat. Unfortunately, about thirty-five minutes before landing, the flight attendant made my dad adjust my seat and that woke me up. After a very long day of travel and after being forcibly awakened, I cried. And I cried, and I cried.

My parents consoled me as best as they could, but I didn't stop until touchdown. Thankfully it was the final thirty minutes of the flight and I didn't keep people from sleeping. My parents were mortified that they were disturbing other people, but most of the faces around were sympathetic. The "crying baby" scenario can scare most people away from flying.

Athena is happy when she flies; this time from Frankfurt to home.

That was the only time that happened and it was a series of circumstances that worked up to it. Many parents are worried about traveling with their children, and that especially applies to parents of special-needs children. A lot of kids in my special school have never been on planes. I am a little world traveler, though. As of this writing, I have been to eighteen different countries. I love to fly because my parents got me used to a routine. And I know at the end of the ride I will be in a place where I am going to have fun and there will be no school.

When we get to the airport, I love to look out the window at the parked planes at the gate. When we board, I always get the window seat. I board the plane, I climb to my seat, and I take my shoes off to get comfortable. I sit back and look out the window and patiently wait for takeoff. My favorite part is the takeoff. I love going super fast! During the flight, I also know that it's an extended snack time, and when I need to, I'll put my shoes on to go to the bathroom.

Don't keep your kids to super strict dietary rules during a flight unless there is some sort of medical concern. Make sure you're loaded with all sorts of treats that your kids are into. Also make sure that you fill your phones and their devices with new content—games, videos, and apps—so they can be entertained. Bring puzzles, activity books, etc. Make sure their time is occupied and it will be an easier trip for you and for everyone on the plane.

And keep their seat belts on the whole time. We have seen kids running up and down the aisles of a plane, but turbulence can hit at any point, and a toddler can get severely injured. In fact, when we were little, our parents never let our feet touch the plane's floor. They did not want us to think that we could just get up and run around. We were carried to our seats and to the bathrooms. And it worked; now we always sit comfortably in our seats and eat and watch TV or play our iPads.

RESTAURANTS

I was in a restaurant when I was eight days old. When you travel, you will usually be in more restaurants than when you're at home. Kids need to behave in restaurants. They can ruin other people's experiences when they misbehave, and that's just not fair. There were times when my sister and I would misbehave in a restaurant. When that would happen (and it doesn't happen often), my parents had a simple answer. They would take my sister or me out of the restaurant. If I was crying, my dad would lift me up and take me outside the restaurant until I stopped. If for some reason I wouldn't stop, then we would leave.

Some parents make their kids stand in the corner when they act bad. My mom and dad would have me or my sister stand by a wall outside the restaurant until we stopped doing what we were doing. That was not fun, so I would stop misbehaving quickly so I could sit and eat.

And just because a kid isn't making noise does not mean that they are not infringing on other people's experiences. Once we were in a very grand old restaurant in Italy. It was lunchtime and a lot of business people ate there. The restaurant had a revolving door, and right in front of this door, a little girl had camped out with her entire collection of pony dolls. She was quiet and playing nicely, but this restaurant was not her house. People entering and leaving literally had to step over and around this girl and her toys. And her brother managed to find a toy in the restaurant, an antique coat rack by the same door.

Of course soon after, there was a loud THUD as the rack fell. Thankfully it didn't hit either of the kids. But the kids also kept getting in the ways of the servers holding hot trays of food that could have burned them. The point is that those kids should have been seated at lunch. And if they can't stay in their seats, then it might be time to grab your food to go.

Me and Athena in Athens under the lights of the Parthenon.

BOATS

We love Curaçao, a beautiful island near Aruba in the Southern Caribbean. There is a small island called Klein Curaçao, a tiny strip of beach fifteen miles away that many tour boat operators bring tourists to for the day. (By the way, it's not worth the trip since the beaches on Curaçao are magnificent—you don't need to waste the day traveling that far to a beach filled with tourists and the fumes of boat engines.)

Well, on this two-hour-plus trip to the island, a Dutch family was letting their three kids (an infant, toddler, and seven-year-old) run all over this catamaran we were on. The problem was that the boat had a lot of gaps in the netting and ropes, and it would have been easy for a kid to fall through. On the return trip, as the parents continued their daylong drinking festival in the *back* of the boat, their three kids were wreaking havoc in the *front* of the boat. There was netting to sit on in the front of the boat and these kids turned it into a WWE wrestling ring.

The problem once again was that there were a lot of people trying to comfortably watch the sun and sea. Honeymooning couples, families, etc., were deprived of this beautiful experience because they had to babysit this Dutch family's brood by default. It got so bad that at one point, the infant had crawled to the edge of the boat near an open gap to the water and was literally scooped up by a few passengers.

Me on catamaran netting watching the Aegean Sea.

Finally, a few of the parents on board "discussed" the near-death experience with the kids' parents so they finally reacted. Enjoy vacation, but don't leave it to other people to babysit your kids, unless they're professionals and you're paying them.

FAMILY SWIMMING POOL TIME

This topic can get my parents a little angry. They work hard and want to enjoy a vacation. They want to sit poolside and hear the waves crashing in the background if by the sea, or maybe they just want to sit and relax by the pool. That idyllic, peaceful scene can be easily broken up by a screaming kid at the pool. Or maybe even a dozen screaming kids at the pool.

Many resorts now have adult pools and then family pools for kids. That separation is a good idea, but it only benefits those without kids. My sister and I love playing in the pool; we swim, splash, and have fun, *but* we don't scream, and we don't bother other people when we are in the pool. Maybe we want to sometimes, but our parents watch us the entire time that we are in the pool. The pool is not our babysitter.

For my sister's fifth birthday, we stayed at a beautiful small resort on the Greek island of Naxos. Villa Marandi Suites was family run and had about fifteen rooms. It had a beautiful pool surrounded by the hotel's small bar and restaurant area; by the way, this restaurant and bar was only open to hotel guests. The place was filled with families, honeymooners, and older couples. After three days of bliss at this beautiful resort, our world almost came crashing or splashing down.

An older British couple was enjoying themselves at one end of the pool, swimming and sipping on gin and tonics. My family came to the shallow end and were quietly enjoying ourselves. That solace soon ended for all. Three American families had just checked in that morning, slept off their jet lag, and proceeded to attack the pool like they had never seen one before. (My dad said it looked like the scene in *Caddyshack* when it was caddie day at the pool.) Each couple had two kids and while the men went to the bar, the women and their kids just repeatedly jumped in and out of the pool while yelling and carelessly splashing people all around.

Cordis Beijing Hotel pool—bathing caps required.

This hotel had no lifeguard; it was a small family run hotel. If these families wanted to go crazy in a pool and splash and scream as they were, there were plenty of villas or houses that they could have rented for a similar price where they could do whatever they wanted in their own pool. But this hotel was not the place for their behavior because their actions diminished the fun for the other guests.

My dad talked to the families about the splashing, but given their brunch of rum cocktails, they were a bit argumentative. Tempers eventually subsided and the owner settled the issue by threatening to ban them from the pool; his case was made easier by the three other sets of hotel guests who confirmed the bad behavior.

Why do people think it's OK to just let children scream at the top of their lungs or shout across the length of a pool? Let the kids have fun. If they want to splash, make sure they don't hit the people around them. If they want to throw a ball, make sure they don't hit the people around them. Be careful! With all this bad behavior, sometimes the victimized guests might start hitting back at the people around them. (Legal disclaimer: My family does not recommend violence as a solution to problems.)

Athan

Eating Right

My family lives to eat. On my iPad, one of my favorite things is to watch cooking videos. Now at eight years old, I am a budding little pastry chef with Athan's and Mom's help. My dad started cooking when he was ten years old, and he still does. He makes yummy food. Mom went to cooking school and worked in restaurants for a very long time before she had me. When I was eight days old, I was in my first restaurant, just like my brother was a few years before me. So take it from an expert; I know about food.

Papou, my dad's dad, was not a good eater. On a vacation to Puerto Rico, he showed us how he ate. One night there, we went to a famous steak restaurant for dinner. Papou ordered lobster ravioli. He then complained that it wasn't great. The next day, we went forty-five minutes east of San Juan to Luquillo, a place known for restaurants with fresh seafood right on the beach. Of course, Papou ordered the steak and complained about it later.

Here's the deal: when in Rome, do as the Romans do. If you're at a steakhouse, order steak. If you're sitting by the beach and the restaurant is getting fresh local fish every morning, don't order the steak. Order what's fresh, but also order what the restaurant is known for, especially when you're traveling.

Both my parents are foodies. They live to eat, not eat to live. My dad is a big man, but my mom, who is athletic and slender, can eat more than he can sometimes. They enjoy tasting new things. But they're also both smart. They research the restaurants that we go to beforehand, and they talk to the servers about the food.

Because of their knowledge, the server often recognizes that my parents are related to the food business in some way. A lot of times, the servers ask my parents if they have worked in restaurants or if they're chefs. (My mom was a general manager, server, and bartender, and my dad has been a chef.) But even without this background, friendly, polite foodies will often get better treatment. Oftentimes, the restaurant or the servers will reward your interest with free drinks, free tastings, or free desserts. In fact, in the majority of meals that my parents have, something is usually given to them for free.

One of the best times they had happened before I came around. My parents went to Cabo San Lucas and were eating at a restaurant in one of the resorts. They had a great meal and had a detailed conversation with the server about the food there and the wine. At one point, the server brought the executive chef out and they started to talk to him about the products and the meal. The chef mentioned that he had a fresh caught tuna that came in to the restaurant a little too late to be put onto the menu for the night.

He then went back to the kitchen and cranked out three amazing tuna sashimi courses with this extremely fresh tuna, including the belly—toro. He joined my parents for each course, paired with proper wines, and it was all for free. Some people say knowledge is power, but sometimes knowledge can just be yummy too.

I love my Parisian restaurants.

RESERVATIONS

Given the amount of information that is now out there regarding restaurants—Yelp, Zagat, Michelin, Tripadvisor—there is no reason to go unprepared into your trip. You don't necessarily have to plan out every meal, but there are probably going to be some places worth planning for. If that's the case make reservations in advance.

This trip might be the only time that you will ever be in this city in your life. Why not make sure that you get to see *that* famous restaurant and experience the food and the scene? Sometimes the hotel concierge may not be able to get last-minute reservations. And a lot of times, the luck of the draw on a random walk may not give you the meal that you're looking for. Sometimes in a foreign destination, it's hard to pass up a nice sign written in English advertising well-known dishes, but in most of those cases, the places usually won't be that good.

In most major US cities, it can be very difficult to just walk into a restaurant and get a table without a reservation; the same is true outside the country. This point is not necessarily going to be true if you're walking along the beach on a Greek island in the summer past restaurant after restaurant along the sea; however, if you're in Athens and want a view of the Acropolis while eating outside, please make a reservation. It can leave you with a very special memory.

Don't be intimidated by the process either. Many places are on websites like OpenTable, others have websites in English in which you can make the reservations directly. And even if it may be intimidating, you can actually call many places to reserve. With Google Translate, it's pretty easy to tell or email someone that you want a reservation for four at 8:00 p.m. on July 10, 2021. And don't forget to say thank you, merci, gracias, etc. In the picture below, we reserved a table outside by the water, in case my duckie needed a bath.

This is me in Piraeus, Athens. Was Athens named after me?

DINING SOLO

This next subject is a tricky one. If you're traveling solo, it's easy to sit in your hotel room, order room service, and watch some TV. The problem with that is that you're not really experiencing the best food in the area, but you're also paying way more than you should for mediocre hotel food. Some people might be a little more adventurous and head downstairs to the hotel restaurant. Ultimately that is definitely more social, but the food in the hotel is usually overpriced and standard. Why not go out solo?

I know that it's scary. My brother and I can't do it because we always have our friends: my pilot bear Amelia Bearhardt, and his bear, Philbin. Plus my parents don't let me out to eat alone; I'm eight! But you're a grownup! You're in a different place! Don't be limited to the hotel menu or to what you can carry out with fast food. Go enjoy and eat. Here's some advice.

In the US, most restaurants, and many, many good ones, have bars where you can sit and enjoy full lunch or dinner service. Bars are great places to sit for solo diners, even if you don't drink. Bartenders are closer on hand and usually pay more attention than servers do because of their proximity to you. They will often engage you more in conversation. Typically many bartenders will have been at the job longer and will be extremely knowledgeable about the menu and can guide you through your ordering process. If you sit with a full meal with a friendly bartender, you're also more likely to get a free drink or dessert as a comp than you would with a server.

Another plus about sitting at the bar is that there are often televisions at the bar, so you have something to watch and look interested in as you're eating. And if you're a bit more social, there are usually other people at the bar.

Bars are great, but in Asia and particularly in Europe, many restaurants don't have full-service bars to eat at. So this next step does take a little courage, but you're traveling so do it. Go to a restaurant and proudly ask for a table for one. Sit and enjoy the views, particularly when you're in a nice outdoor square (piazza) in Italy. There may not be a television, but there will be nonstop street theater of all kinds with the people that you see. Bring a book, an iPad, or your phone and get on the restaurant's Wi-Fi. Or bring a crossword puzzle if you want to be sure that you have something to do. If on a work trip, bring some work; just don't get any sauce on it from the pasta.

There are also many food markets across the world, and a lot are growing in the States. Markets are great because they're geared to small groups and solo travelers. In Barcelona's *Boqueria* or the *Mercado de San Miguel* in Madrid, it's easy to wait for a seat or a spot at the bar and you can order away and feast on stellar food and drink. You won't get what they have there in the hotel room!

Remember, part of the travel experience is the food. Don't miss out on eating because you were a bit scared and embarrassed to dine alone. It's more accepted in foreign destinations anyway. My dad used to travel solo a lot and he always went to great restaurants. Even for dinner, you can enjoy amazing food and a nice night out. Many restaurants have half bottles of wine or really nice by-the-glass options so you don't have to order a bottle. Or order a bottle and have a nice long meal. The choice is yours.

Athena

CHAPTER NINETEEN

Sometimes You Gotta Splurge III

Universal Studios is amazing. Both the one in Orlando and the one in Hollywood have amazing rides and attractions. They're both pretty expensive, but if you're going to go, I would suggest looking at their VIP tours. They may seem way more expensive, but then we have that concept of value again.

So here's the story....A few years ago, we went to Universal Studios Hollywood. It was in January, so the regular admission price would have been in the $450 range for the four of us. The VIP price was about $1,200. I get it; it's a big difference in price, but....

The VIP experience was great. When we pulled into the park, we pulled right to the closest parking lot and a valet parked the car. This service was included with VIP.

We were a little early for our tour, so we entered through the VIP entrance (no line) and went to the lounge where a lovely breakfast buffet was available. We had a beautiful breakfast and soon began our guided VIP tour.

Our guide led our small group of about fifteen people to our custom tram for the studio tour. In contrast, the regular ticket has a large tram with close to one hundred people on it. Our bus was very comfortable, and water bottles were provided, so we didn't have to pay at the stands in the park. Also the VIP studio tour does a number of behind-the-scene tours that the regular ticket does not get to access. We were allowed to walk around some sets, and we got to see the props department among other perks.

After we spent the morning doing the studio thing, we came back to the ride side of the park and had a wonderful buffet for lunch at the VIP-only restaurant. And the food was delicious. It was a full buffet including a great dessert selection that easily would have been anywhere from $40 to $75 a person if it were available inside the park.

After lunch, we regathered and skipped the lines to take our VIP seats for the *Waterworld* show. It was great, and we had perfect views from the center. When the show ended, we spent the rest of the day going to every ride in the park. We did not wait on any lines. We were always escorted right to the front as we went through the VIP entrances. Since it was a holiday, the lines were long, even in January.

At the end of the day, we were tired, but we got our value from the ticket. We went on every ride in the park, and some we did twice. In our nine-hour day, we saw and did everything. Many people come to the park and only are able to do a few rides and attractions because of the wait times; they almost need to come back to experience more because so much of the time is spent on line waiting.

My parents also did the VIP at Universal Orlando for Halloween Horror Nights. There were nine haunted houses, and my parents went to them all and got to ride everything. Some of the regular wait times for the houses that night were close to three hours.

Bang for your buck is the idea here. Paying a few hundred to go on two rides? Or pay a bit more to go on everything and not have to wait providing value? If you're really a fan and can afford the splurge, it means you can probably wait a couple of years before returning to the park because when you were there, you did it all.

*That's Me and Poppy from Trolls at Universal
Studios Hollywood.*

CHAPTER TWENTY

Beware the Night (Flights)

"*Caveat emptor*" is a Latin phrase that means let the buyer beware. Sometimes when you're shopping for flights, you will notice a cheaper fare, and then get a quick brushback to reality when you see the strange time for the flight. For instance, a lot of low-budget European carriers have 11:00 p.m. to 3:00 a.m. flights. Well, that works OK with a backpack but may not be so great for families. What are you going to do with your luggage that whole time after you leave your hotel? Checkout time at most hotels is from 11:00 a.m. to 1:00 p.m. Where are you going to shower? Also when you get to your destination at 4:00 a.m., what are you supposed to do? Hotel check-in times tend to be from 2:00 p.m. to 4:00 p.m.

Don't automatically jump on the flight because the price looks great. Factor the spending on food and the inconvenience of having to kill time before your room is ready. Some might suggest doing some sightseeing, but at 4:00 a.m., most sites are closed. Plus your kids will hate history forever if you take them on a predawn walking tour of Rome or Athens when they're worn out from a late-night flight.

Another thing to be wary of is on the flight itself. Getting on a plane at 11:00 p.m. can mean that some people were hitting the bar or airport lounge pretty hard before boarding. We just got back from a late flight from Fort Lauderdale to New York City, and it was not fun listening to the drunk girl behind using her air sickness bag for fifteen minutes, and the smell was even worse.

Also these flights screw up the natural body clocks of kids. Don't be surprised if you have a crying baby as the soundtrack for the flight. Given that these might be the last flights of the night, these flights are often delayed. Think about it: these planes are bussing from airport to airport during the day; any delay somewhere along the way usually gets bumped along to the next flight and next and so on. By the time the last flight is ready to go, it probably is going to be running late. And during those delays, your fellow passengers can have an extra drink at the bar—oh wait, is that vomiting drunk girl?

Now some red-eye flights (love that name) are logical, like East Coast flights to Europe. Get on in the evening, watch some TV, try to sleep a few hours, and wake up in Europe. Some of the West Coast to East Coast red-eyes can be quiet too, but watch your destinations and times of year. The spring break red eye from Vegas to New York City might not be too quiet.

Athan

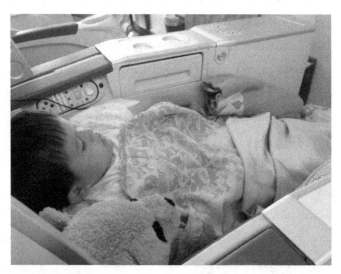

Slept in a full bed for most of the fourteen-hour flight from Los Angeles to Seoul, South Korea, on an A380 in business class with a reduced price ticket!

CHAPTER TWENTY-ONE

European Travel

Most people who travel within the United States and stay in hotels have a similar picture of a hotel room; the room will have either one or two beds, there is usually a small table area with a chair or two, some type of shelf or counter with a television set, and a bathroom and sink area. These types of rooms come in all types of sizes and with various levels of luxury depending on the hotel brand.

Most of the time, the rooms range from about 275 to 600 square feet. For spring break or a trip to Vegas, it's not unheard of to sleep six to eight friends together. Or when people are on the road in a bigger group, maybe they will pile into a room for a night to save some money and get some rest.

However, European hotels are different. The rooms are generally smaller...much smaller. Try using the sites that show you the size. Remember they use square meters (10 square meters are about 108 square feet). The beds are smaller…much smaller. Two friends traveling together in Europe might have to split up their twin beds (really, two single beds put side by side).

The electricity in the rooms is often activated by a room key card. There is usually a slot by the door on the inside of your room where you can insert your key card to keep the power going. This tidbit is important information if you're in Southern Europe in the summer when it's really hot. Your room will be an oven when you return.

The Europeans are very environmentally conscious, which is admirable, but when on vacation and returning from a long day of sightseeing in heat, we would like to relax in a cold room. Some parents might want to get two keys and leave one in the power slot. Just saying! European hotels will ask for your passports when you check in. This policy is standard, and they will give them back to you after they take your information.

Some older hotels that still use metallic keys will ask that you leave the key at the desk when you leave. This practice is an older one, but it's safe. Also these places tend to have really big cumbersome keys that almost force you to leave them.

European hotels will generally know how many people are in your room. In other words, if you're a family of four and you only put two guests on your reservation, then there may be trouble. They might make you pay more, or more importantly, you might not be able to stay in the room because of various regulations, no matter how big the room is. *Make sure that you book your rooms for the appropriate number of guests with the right ages.* You might have to pay more, but this is generally unavoidable. You might be able to get away with sneaking some people in to some of the larger chain hotels in some big cities but generally not, especially in smaller towns and in smaller hotels.

Also some hotels may not allow overnight "guests." Following up on the same policy, there are a number of hotels, especially in some resort towns or islands, that do not allow guests to stay over. Check the hotel policy if you think you might be making friends.

European bathrooms often have showers that have openings and no curtain. Bathrooms are expected to get wet and many have drains and toilet paper covers for these occurrences. Others may just have glass or plastic walls that only cover half of the shower or tub. They also use hand-held nozzles more often so be careful of the spray and don't get the whole room wet. European bathrooms also have bidets. Don't treat it like a sink, toilet, or a water fountain. If you're going to use it, use it to wash up your bottom.

On the very plus side, almost all European hotel rooms include very nice breakfast spreads with coffees, tea, juices, cold cuts, cheeses, eggs, sausages, fruits, breads, and pastries. The elevators or "lifts" will often be quite small and slow. It will be hard to get all of your luggage inside. You might have to take more than one ride.

Often times the heat and the air-conditioning will not be what you're used to. Sometimes that is just the way it is. If it's an unbearable thought, you might want to read the reviews and pay extra for an assured icebox of a room.

Be careful of flushing the toilet with too much paper. US pipes tend to be bigger, and the pressure is stronger with the flush, so flush often and use less paper. On some small islands in Greece, for instance, you might even see signs by the toilet that suggest throwing the used toilet paper in the trash. Now this thought disgusts me a bit so we just make sure to really use small amounts of paper only and flush more. And use that bidet! *Beware the wet wipes*! They will cause floods for sure in most places if you flush them.

The televisions will also be different. Many will be older and not all HD. Also there will be naked people on television; later at night there might be commercials with naked girls. And cursing. Also they will not always have channels in English. The few that they may have in English will be the BBC, CNN, or some other news outlet. Remember that you didn't come to Europe to sit in a hotel room watching TV.

On that note, your Netflix and other streaming services on your phone and computer may not work in different countries, so if you're addicted to a big show you might need to figure out something. One time we were away when the season finale of *Game of Thrones* was scheduled. Our hotel was supposed to have HBO, but it didn't. Our parents were so desperate that they actually transferred us to another hotel for the night just to see the show. And we got a mini-vacation on vacation to a different pool and beach.

These hotels are also going to be notorious about checkout and check-in times, so please plan accordingly. A few summers ago, we were going to be in Athens for two days, and we got there at 8:00 a.m. We were already dressed in our touring clothes, and we got to the hotel in the morning *expecting* to put our bags in storage so that we could go out and enjoy the day as opposed to waiting in the hotel lobby for countless hours complaining that our room wasn't ready.

SIESTA, SIESTA

There is a tradition that is sadly dying away in Southern Europe—the siesta. Siesta is a Spanish term for afternoon rest. It's common in Southern Mediterranean countries like Spain, France, Italy, and Greece. The siesta time is from around 3pm to 7pm when a number of businesses close down. They do this to go home to family, to nap, or to avoid the oppressive heat of the afternoon sun in summer.

This time period is another great time to live like a local, both if you're with family or if you're young party travelers. The typical family gets up early, does breakfast, and then goes sightseeing or is at the pool or beach until lunch then repeats the routine. Even if your kids are not typically nappers, the jet lag and busy days will help them and they may welcome the rejuvenation that a nap can provide. That hot sun can knock your kids out. It may do the same to you. You can join them for naps or maybe have some private time together while they nap.

In any case, since most of the stores are closed, it's not the best time to be out walking around anyway. Additionally, you will be prepared for your evening meal since in these countries, dinner is typically served very late, partially because its cooler when the sun is down late but also because people have rested.

Even if you're single party travelers, the siesta can make sense if you will be up late in the Euro clubs. You can always siesta poolside to get that sun, but some down-time can really help you later on.

Athan and Athena

CHAPTER TWENTY-TWO

Red Light & Red Flags

This is Athan and Athena's dad; they're too young for these chapters. In a lot of amazing places around the world, including some here in the States, there are different standards of morality than you might be used to.

For example, in Madrid, right in the middle of a very popular tourist area, there is a major street that connects two other major streets. If you happen to take this major pedestrian route, you might be surprised to see the dozens of scantily clad women lining both sides of the block. They will be fully dressed, but they will be dressed like they're going out to a dance club. Keep in mind this will be true at 11:00 a.m., 3:00 p.m., and 2:00 a.m. These women are sex workers. If you do happen to be walking on a street like this in any city, don't worry, they will tend to ignore the families. Just have an answer ready in case your kids ask you what the girls are doing hanging around. "Well, there is a movie getting filmed, I think…"

On that note, we all know that "what happens in Vegas, stays in Vegas." Let's talk about Vegas a bit. If you're in town for a few days, maybe with some friends, maybe with a partner, or maybe solo for a convention, this scenario can happen to you. You're sitting alone at a nice hotel bar, waiting for your friend or just having a drink. Suddenly, despite the bar seats being empty all around, a bathing suit model will sit next to you at the bar and strike up a conversation. Now this is Vegas, and if this situation has happened to you before, this very well might be a model. On the other hand, if this occurrence is a bit irregular, the person may be "working." Just be aware.

Many of us have heard of the famous red-light district in Amsterdam. Other cities across the world have "red light" areas that are pretty well-known, so if you choose to you can either steer clear or visit. Many of these places are interesting to see even from a taxi or on a quick walk on through. Again, when you're with your family, exercise your own discretion. But keep in mind that even though there are "red light" zones in many places, there are also strip clubs in plain sight mixed in with retail stores, restaurants, hotels, etc. And for those who enjoy the occasional visit to a "gentlemen's club," many of these clubs in the rest of the world will be very similar to the clubs in the States in many ways; however, in many countries these clubs are also brothels. And many of the ones that are not brothels are still places where one can "rent" company for the evening. Just keep this information in mind.

Another thing to consider is that standards of nudity and dress are different abroad than they are at home. It's a normal occurrence to have topless women at pools and at the beaches, and thongs for women and speedos for men often make for a full moon sighting, or two, when you're poolside. You do not have to join in on the fun, but you may get a sight. If you're very much averse to this, you can call or email your hotel in advance to find out about their pool policy, but at many beaches, people may be hanging out, literally. Do a quick online search about your beach if this is an issue.

Also be wary of your foreign television channels. Especially at night, certain channels that may have had normal programming in the day will play risqué films, or even with standard television shows, they will have X-rated commercials for sex services. Sometimes if you decide to order the kids a pay-per-view movie, it also may unlock multiple pay channels, including porn. Take a quick look before you attack that remote.

JK

CHAPTER TWENTY-THREE

Don't Get Taken at Your Hotel

In *Taken 1, 2,* and *3* and I think it may be up to *Taken 12* at this point—Liam Neeson utters his famous line that goes something like "I have a certain set of skills that I have taken a lifetime to build up." His skills were special forces/ninja-type stuff: mine are travel based, like knowing what a rip-off is and not being taken by it.

Minibars look great. What's not to like? A full selection of yummy drinks, often accompanied by even more tempting snacks—except all these treats are marked up by hundreds of percent! Healthy organic kale chips for $12 a bag? Pringles for $8? Water for $10? Water? And let's not even talk about the wines and alcoholic beverages.

Casino mogul Steve Wynn famously did not put minibars into many of his big casino hotel rooms, like the beautiful Bellagio in Las Vegas. His policy was even parodied in one of the *Ocean's Eleven* movies, when Daniel Ocean told the casino magnate "Minibar." Wynn knew he would make more profit when the guests ventured downstairs to the casino floor; that's why they serve free alcohol when you play. However, most hotels don't have casinos, and they know that minibars are a cash cow.

I know that you're on vacation and if you want to splurge on a late night *Toblerone* bar then good for you. I'm just saying know what you're getting into. There are price lists for these minibars, but they're usually hidden somewhere.

Another place to get taken is the hotel gift shop. When you go somewhere warm and sunny with pools and beaches you might want to bring your own tanning products. If not, you will be paying two to three times more than it would cost in a typical drugstore. Same for diapers, wet wipes, swimmies, bug spray, etc. If possible, make a run with your car or even cab (it's still likely to be much cheaper) to an outside store to stock up. And while you're at it, grab some water bottles. Or pack your own stuff and bring it with you. Just be sure it's not in your carry-on bag. Be wary of hotel prices so that you're not surprised at checkout with a $60 bill for that room service burger and beer.

JK

In Grand Cayman, Athena shows you what she thinks of rip-offs.

CHAPTER TWENTY-FOUR

Casinos

Casinos can be fun. A casino can literally make or break your trip. You could leave and your entire vacation could be paid for, or on the other side of things, it could cost double or worse.

If you're already a gambler, then at this point, you hopefully know your own limits and games to play, etc. Good luck and enjoy yourself. For the beginners, have a little fun. Give yourself a limit and start at the cheaper games and tables. Get the free drinks; enjoy the "interesting" people you will meet.

Foreign casinos will often require that you bring your passports. They also often have a minor admission fee that usually includes a free drink or a chip to gamble with. Many hotels and concierges may have passes for free entry. Also many foreign casinos may have dress codes so you might want to check in on that. Also like in the States, different casinos have different rules for games, so maybe observe for a while before diving in.

If you know that you're going to play for a while and you're going to be gambling a decent amount, tell the casino that you want a players card. These cards rack points based on your bets and length of stay. By the end of a trip, your daily blackjack game might well earn you a discounted or free stay the next time you return. You can even book the room through the casino host at many casino hotels, so give it a roll. Who knows where the dice might fall?

JK

CHAPTER TWENTY-FIVE

Where Are the Lawyers?

America is the land of the lawyers. There are more lawyers here than almost anywhere else. And people like to sue. Sue, sue, sue.

In America, there are signs giving warning about every little possibility. Hiking near the forests in Alaska? There will be a sign about grizzly bears. Swimming in the ocean? Beware the sharks and currents. Drinking a soda? Beware the cancer-causing chemicals. Taking a medicine? Beware the side effects. You get the idea.

Anyway, it doesn't seem like the rest of the world has this American tradition. The rest of the world couldn't care less if we were silly enough to jump off our sightseeing boat in South Africa that is looking for great white sharks. They don't care if we trip on two-thousand-year-old steps to an ancient fortress. There won't be fences to stop you from falling off the cliff by that same fortress. So be careful. Be aware of your surroundings, and use common sense to avoid injury. Try not to be that person who spends a few vacation days in a hospital and returns with a cast.

And don't think if that were to happen, you will be able to sue somebody for it. Chances are that if it happened abroad, you will be to blame, or at least to their governing body you will be. Be safe and travel smart.

JK

CHAPTER TWENTY-SIX

Crime, Corruption, and Terrorism

My family and I have done our best to stay safe during our travels. Thankfully there have been no big thefts or personal threats to our safety. But here are a few tales:

Just the change—In Hungary, many years ago, I got into a taxi cab and took a ride from a restaurant to my hotel. At the end of the ride, I paid the driver, even throwing in a little tip, and went back to my room. The next morning, I realized that the driver paid me back in another country's lesser-valued currency. In the end, I lost about $30 worth of currency. It could have been a lot worse. Moral of the story: just because the money looks like it's from a Monopoly game, it's not all the same. Make sure it's legitimate and pay attention to shopkeepers and other cashiers when you're paying for things.

Crime can happen anywhere and often does. Be mindful of your bags everywhere. Don't leave your wallet or cards on counters. Don't be distracted. There is a great scam in Italy in which the local criminal "entrepreneurs" throw a fake baby at you and when you rush to grab it, their partners make off with your bag or purse. There's also the good old smash-your-car window and take your bags when you're still in the car.

Don't park your cars with your suitcases or bags in them. Most criminals know what the rental car license plates look like, or they will see the bags and think of them as a target of opportunity. Be wise. Use the safes in your hotel rooms. Also don't bring your most expensive watch when you're traveling. Don't be ostentatious in areas with extreme poverty. Just be mindful of your surroundings and be aware. Be safe.

The Manila Shakedown—On our trip to Manila in 2014, we got into a taxi at a very secure five-star hotel. We were taking a six-minute trip to another hotel where the rest of our family was staying. A few blocks later, the taxi driver inexplicably made the wrong turn toward a police roadblock. When the police pulled him over, the police explained, in English, that unless I paid the "fine," the driver would be tossed in jail, and the car would be impounded. I politely said that was not my concern, but the police then said we would all be brought to the station and held as witnesses, etc. I realized that this was an impromptu "toll booth." We paid the officer $50 for the fine and went on our way. The driver did not get a tip when he dropped us off as he undoubtedly was in on the scam with the local police.

A few days later, our Filipino cousin, one who lives in Manila, ran into a similar situation as he was driving by a major intersection. The road police cited him for a "minor violation" in their eyes. He was able to get out of the ticket and any trouble with a quick deposit of $100 to Manila's finest. Thankfully this corruption is being combatted more in the Philippines, but it's just the way of life in many countries.

While driving from Santo Domingo to Samana in the beautiful Dominican Republic on the newly paved highway connecting the regions, we were stopped for speeding by two young motorcycle police. We had two fluent-in-Spanish Cubans with us, and we were able to go on after a $25 "gift." Be careful, and have some cash on hand but not too much. In these situations, there is not much one can do other than to be polite and firm.

Terrorism—We have been in Europe at the same time that some horrific acts of terror took place. These crimes against humanity deter many people from travel, but they shouldn't. We live in Manhattan in Chelsea. A few years ago, a man put a bomb right next to one of our favorite restaurants. Thankfully nobody was killed, and he was caught and thrown in jail. Another time, a man drove a van and mowed down bikers and runners by the river, less than a mile from our house. And from our old apartment in Brooklyn, we could see the beautiful Freedom Tower being built out of the ruins of the Twin Towers.

I know that many people do not live in places where terror has happened and that is the point. Life must go on. Be cautious. Kabul, Afghanistan, in the spring may not be a great first overseas trip, but if you're very concerned, there are plenty of places that are very safe. When you spend money to go away, you should enjoy your travels, not spend the time being worried.

JK

CHAPTER TWENTY-SEVEN

Travel[ed] like Us in Mexico

We just got back from one of our best vacations ever. We spent nine days at the Fairmont Mayakoba near Cancún, Mexico for Christmas. This vacation was extra special because it was the longest gap between flights (August 2019—December 2020) for Athan and Athena. We are lucky that we get to travel so much and that we enjoy doing it. We thought about it and researched a lot before choosing a place to go on vacation in a resurgent COVID world.

The Fairmont took great care to make sure the staff was always masked and sanitizers were everywhere, and we felt comfortably distanced from other guests at all times. Most of the time, we were completely alone in the beautiful water. The hotel was at about 50 percent capacity, and it felt like we had it to ourselves most days.

That trip illustrated a lot of the lessons from this book. We paid 40 percent less for this trip than we would have normally, especially during the high season, and the hotel was half empty. We had an issue in one of the restaurants on the second night, and we sent an email to the general manager, who quickly and professionally resolved the situation in a way that was beneficial to us and to his staff.

We decided to splurge and pay a little extra to go on a private boat to go snorkeling instead of being with other guests. On the boat, it was all open air, and the two-person crew had their masks on. Similarly, we used the top-rated car service from Tripadvisor to arrange for a private car to and from the hotel as opposed to sharing a shuttle with others. We weren't being antisocial; we were just trying to be as careful as possible in the age of COVID.

In the car, the driver was masked, as were we, and we kept the windows open the whole time. We chose to eat every delicious meal outdoors, and unlike most of our trips, we never left the gated property. (It included four hotels and residences). It was a great trip, even more so after this crazy year.

JK

At the Fairmont Mayakoba in Mexico, safety was paramount.

CHAPTER TWENTY-EIGHT

Post-COVID

People are born wanting to travel; the proof of that is that people moved all around the Earth from the place we all originally came from. It's in our DNA to travel. Hopefully, the near future will see the end of COVID and we all can burst out of our lockdowns. When we do, remember that we can never be too smart when it comes to travel…so please, if you want to have a great trip and save a few dollars along the way…

Travel like Us.

Jason Karameros

Athan and Athena Karameros

Follow us on Instagram @AthanandAthena

Athan and Athena at the Cordis Hotel in Hong Kong.

The end for now; we will travel some more and chat again!

ABOUT THE AUTHOR

Jason Karameros has been an educational consultant and private tutor for over 20 years. An Ivy League educated native New Yorker, he still lives in Manhattan with his wife, two children, and their puppy, Truffle. He is an avid traveler and normally spends more than two months a year exploring the world. He enjoys wine and cocktails, cooking at home, and dining out. A gastronome as well as fitness buff, he lives to "Travel, eat, work out, repeat!"